Kaizen

How to Apply Lean Kaizen to Your Startup Business and Management to Improve Productivity, Communication, and Performance

Kaizen

Table of Contents

Introduction

Thanks for purchasing this book, *Kaizen: How to Apply Lean Kaizen to Your Startup Business and Management to Improve Productivity, Communication, and Performance*. This book expounds the Japanese concept and contains a comprehensive guide on how to apply it in managing your startup.

More than half of startups fail within 10 years after their launch. This fact remains true regardless of how good or bad the economy is. Poor management is one of the top reasons behind the said phenomenon.

Starting Is Easier than Before

These days, it only takes guts for some people to start a venture. Besides, generating business ideas isn't that much of a problem when you can simply search and copy online. Or, you can visit the nearest commercial district and discover what essential product or service is missing.

When it comes to getting funds, you can find another work and save your income from that. You can also sell your own things online and on a garage sale. Borrowing money from family and friends is another option. Don't forget taking loans from banks or lenders. You can try crowdfunding as well.

What about land and equipment? Well, you don't have to buy everything at once. You also don't need brand-new equipment. If location matters in your business, you can rent for the meantime. In case your offer can be provided online, you can work anywhere as long as your computer is connected to the Internet.

Downloadable and web-based programs make it easy to perform functions like planning and accounting. There are also available templates that you can use to create proposals and contracts. If you don't know how to operate the programs or what to include in the documents, you can just search for guides online. When you start your business, you can practically do all tasks on your own.

Getting Your First Customer

Creating a social media page for your business doesn't cost a thing. You won't even waste precious time for it. You can do it while waiting in line, riding the subway or relaxing in your couch. Yet, doing so allows you to promote your business for free.

Several tasks involved in operating a startup are easier and cheaper than ever. Consequently, the competition is fiercer as aspiring entrepreneurs take the plunge every now and then. As a result, getting the attention of prospects is more challenging than before. How are you going to draw your first customer then?

Novelty and curiosity could lure your first set of customers. However, you can't depend on those two factors as time goes by. What will you do next?

Managing Your Business

Whether your launch succeeds or fails, you're bound to think about your next move. It's the first step in improving. Planning and implementing improvements form part of good management. Furthermore, good management strikes a balance between learning from the past, implementing changes in the present, and preparing for the future.

Improvement is both a way and an end-goal in managing a business. How does that make sense?

Introducing Kaizen

Kaizen is originally a Sino-Japanese word denoting improvement. As it got adapted into western use, the meaning evolved into continuous improvement. The qualifier isn't just a fancy addition though.

Continuous improvement and respect for people summed up the guidelines known as The Toyota Way. Published in 2001, the guidelines were sought and studied by western entrepreneurs, managers and even political leaders. All of them hoped to learn how one Asian company became one of the frontrunners in a market dominated by North American companies.

As a startup owner myself, I was eager to learn from successful companies like Toyota. I wasn't alone in feeling that way. I know you're also curious, and so are other aspiring entrepreneurs who want to be prepared before they begin operating their businesses.

This isn't the first book discussing management lessons from Toyota. However, this stands out for making the said lessons appropriate for running a startup. It doesn't shy away from discussing the challenges that make kaizen difficult to apply.

You see, The Toyota Way stresses good relationship between managers and subordinates. However, that doesn't seem valuable when you're outsourcing instead of hiring your own employees.

Outsourcing is beneficial in many ways, especially for startups. It's cheaper than hiring full-time employees because you don't have to pay for monthly salaries and benefits. You don't need to spend time on recruitment. Without employees, you won't deal with labor disputes and office politics as well.

As your startup grows, however, you can't rely on outsourcing alone. You have to stop doing everything on your own so you can devote your time and skills on important functions. Sooner or later, you'll require talented people to help you improve your venture.

Administrative and marketing assistants usually comprise the first hires of a startup. Next, you'll get employees in-charge of operating and maintaining your equipment. If you're providing services, you'll need specialists to further get ahead. Even if your startup is about selling digital products and services, you're going to make a technical team as you expand.

As you open another branch, you'll need a new set of employees. Who makes an ideal manager for the new branch? Between a qualified applicant and a long-time employee, the latter tends to be more preferable.

Why? Hiring in-house boosts employee morale. After all, the promotion can serve as recognition of hard work and loyalty.

It also saves time. Your long-time employee doesn't need a lengthy orientation before handling his or her new job. If you hire someone else, you'll have to introduce him or her to your company values, vision, and culture first.

Going back to managing a startup, better funding and equipment can get you ahead of the pack. However, topnotch human resource is one of the biggest factors that gets you far. You can read a lot of books and attend many classes. Yet, it's still more time-efficient to hire people and hone their skills as you improve yours.

Continuous improvement begins with the leader and subordinates. Get to know how it happens with the help of this book on kaizen.

Chapter 1: Demystifying Kaizen

"Open the window over there and take a look. It's a big world out there." (Sakichi Toyoda)

By this time, you've probably heard or read about the humble beginnings of well-known companies like Google, Apple, Starbucks, McDonald's, and Kentucky Fried Chicken. Their stories of starting with nothing and changing the world in some ways, as Boitnott (2014) described it, are a great source of inspiration for aspiring and struggling entrepreneurs. However, it's worth noting that all of the said companies started and thrived in the US.

Donilon (2016) asserted that the US had territorial advantage. The same can't be said about other countries that went or are still going through territorial disputes with their neighbors. The said edge was even more evident when the two world wars happened. With vast oceans and countries on its sides, Uncle Sam was practically untouchable.

The US dealt with crises along the way. Yet, it remained politically and economically better than many countries. The stability and positive view on the country helped American entrepreneurs more than they're willing to admit. Can you imagine the challenges that a foreign company faces when it competes on the world market?

The Unconventional Asian Company

For more than 70 years, General Motors was dubbed as the number one automaker in terms of sales. Ford came next and held the position for five decades. However, things changed when Toyota entered the picture in 2008 (Bunkley, 2008).

Founded by Sakichi Toyoda, the Japanese automaker began as a part of a loom-manufacturing company in the 1930s. Aside from automatic looms, Toyoda also introduced and implemented the concept of jidoka (Rosenthal, 2011). Originally meaning automation with a human touch, the said concept would later serve as one of the two pillars of the Toyota Production System. The other pillar was just-in-time and it was developed by Taiichi Ohno, one of Toyota Motor Corporation's industrial engineers.

It was unusual for a company to make concepts for its production system and management approach. However, Toyota made it acceptable. It only reflected the company's creativity and willingness to handle challenges.

From Toyoda's Challenge to an Unprecedented Success

Toyota's success in the automotive industry wasn't earned overnight. In 1937, the Toyota Motor Company was established as an independent entity from Toyoda Automatic Loom Works. Years before that, Sakichi Toyoda initiated a challenge to invent a durable and efficient battery that's dependent on hydropower, not petroleum (Hasegawa, 2008).

Sakichi Toyoda's son, Kiichiro, spearheaded the establishment of the Toyota Motor Company. By the time the younger Toyoda did that, US and Russian-based researchers were already working on innovations for their automobiles.

Toyoda's challenge was given more importance when World War II began. Petroleum supply to Japan became scarce. That time was also difficult for Japanese researchers and their foreign counterparts to exchange ideas.

Without much choice, Toyota solely depended on professors from Japan's top universities. Despite having dozens of experts in one roof, the automaker still failed in creating the battery that Sakichi Toyoda wanted. Nevertheless, the discipline and dedication fostered in the research became instrumental in the development of the company's management approach.

The postwar period almost drove Toyota to bankruptcy in 1949. It survived, thanks to a loan from a consortium of banks. However, the company had to lay off 2,000 employees. Kiichiro Toyoda didn't want to fire employees, but he didn't have much choice as it was stipulated in their loan agreement. He stepped down as president when the mass layoff happened (Assembly, 2007).

Toyota's researchers gradually went back to work on Sakichi Toyoda's challenge. Japan's oil crisis and introduction of emission regulations in the 1970s further served as motivation for the company to innovate.

By 2008, Toyota still failed to accomplish Sakichi Toyoda's challenge. However, the innovations they developed paved the way for hybrid cars. Despite the unprecedented feat, then-company president Katsuaki Watanabe downplayed it and asserted that they're concerned with their automobiles' performance (Hazegawa, 2008)

Innovation, Not Competition

Who doesn't want to be the frontrunner in an industry? Imagine the number of investors lining up to offer you funding. You can finally help more people than before. Above all, the recognition is bound to make you feel good.

However, one of the important lessons you should learn from Toyota is that ranking first shouldn't serve as your main motivation in managing your business. It's true that the Japanese automaker beat Detroit's Big Three (GM, Ford, and Chrysler) in total sales in 2008 (Vlasic, 2011). The success was relatively short-lived, though. In just a couple of years, the American companies reclaimed the throne as their Japanese competitor had to deal with recalls. The rise, fall and return of the Big Three just prove that records are made to be broken.

A few years later, however, Toyota's sales went up and defeated the American automakers again. In fact, it's the number one automaker as of 2017, according to the Organisation Internationale des Constructeurs d'Automobiles. GM and Ford ranked fourth and fifth respectively.

Toyota's secret to success is out in the open. In his book, David Magee (2007) emphasized kaizen (continuous improvement) as one of the factors that helped the Japanese automaker become number one.

The Influence of Oriental Culture on Kaizen

Have you ever visited a nearby Chinatown, K-town or J-town? These Asian communities in foreign lands like the US reflect how tight their ties are. Likewise, they also signify the oriental culture's emphasis on social harmony. When western culture stresses individualism, its eastern counterpart gives more importance to group dynamics. Jeffrey K. Liker and Michael Hoseus (2008) further elaborated the differences of western and eastern cultures in many aspects of managing a business.

Culture played a role in the development of Toyota's management style. Instead of encouraging individuals to do differently, eastern culture dictates to try fitting into a group. Instead of recognizing an individual's accomplishment, it gives credit to teamwork.

Such attitude is beneficial in handling errors in business operations. For Toyota, a problem means deviating from standard while western culture views it as a result of someone's mistake. To manage the problem, the Japanese automaker encourages employees to ask for help. In contrast, western culture lets the individual who made a mistake to take the blame and resolve the issue on his or her own.

Ensuring harmony in the workplace enables kaizen to happen. Employees resolve problems more efficiently when they do it together and when they refuse to pin blame on anyone. By continuously resolving issues, they can improve processes. That's easier said than done though.

The Challenges of Implementing Kaizen

To be clear, you don't have to fully embrace oriental culture to apply kaizen. However, you should be prepared to do adjustments if you want to overcome the biggest challenges in applying the approach.

Resistance is among the hurdles against kaizen (Rodrigues, 2018). While you may warm up to the idea, do you think your employees will? Time will help weed out employees who don't share the same vision as you. However, time won't be enough to overturn how others view kaizen. One way to resolve this is by training your employees about continuous improvement.

Lack of communication tends to trigger and worsen resistance as well. As an employer and a manager, make sure your employees can easily talk to you about problems, suggestions and opinions. Being able to communicate with you helps them become more accepting of your ideas and decisions. Additionally, better communication speeds up crisis management.

Misconceptions are another challenge against the implementation of kaizen in startups. Continuous improvement isn't synonymous to continuous successes. The positive results won't be quick as well.

Be prepared to experience losses as you focus on improving your offer. That's just part of taking risks. Moreover, applying kaizen discourages you from minding the trends. Trends come and go, don't they? Sometimes, they favor other startups and cause yours to lag behind. But at the end of the day, the well-developed product and service take the lead for a longer time.

Failure to define important process is also an obstruction to kaizen's efficiency. In the latter chapters of this book, you'll learn about the types of waste in business operations. Some of the said waste are related to processes.

Three Principles Behind Effective Kaizen

Kaizen's efficiency has a lot to do with its three principles, namely process and results, systematic thinking, and not blaming (Magee, 2007). Under the first principle, both the process and results are considered equally significant. It's important for Toyota to sell well, to make quality cars and to improve their production processes. Think about this: What's the point of being number in sales but also having high operational costs and facing the possibility of recalls?

Process and results affect each other. If there are no problems in your process, you're likely to create polished products or offer refined services. Ideally, that leads to positive results as evident in increased sales and improved brand awareness. Such kind of results can motivate both the management and workforce to keep on doing well. It can also prompt investors to consider funding one of your business proposals.

The second principle, systematic thinking, is all about seeing the big picture. This means you don't just see the problem as it is. Dig deeply and look widely. In the next chapter, you'll find out the root cause analysis that serves as basis for crisis management.

You should also apply this to every action you do for your business. Always consider the short-term and long-term repercussions of every action.

Such principle prevents you from acting recklessly. Thoughtless actions put your startup's reputation at risk. Instead of having one problem, you end up with a lot. You can even cause disruptions in your operations, which can mean losses.

The third principle is something that many managers fail to do: not blaming. Blaming is useless. A lot of people know it but they still do it. Why? It's simply because it's easy to do. It also serves as a blanket excuse for the mistake and bad results.

Blaming wastes time and effort. Instead of using that time and effort to work on the mistakes, you'll end up managing ill feelings and unpleasant atmosphere at work. If that unpleasantness resulted in defects and operational disruptions, you'll deal with additional problems and waste more of your resources.

No matter how grave the error is, don't blame. Communicate with the person who committed the mistake and work things out. Depending on the gravity of the mistake, you may impose sanctions but make sure they're still legal, ethical and proportional to the error.

How to Start Continuous Improvement

Continuous improvement starts somewhere. Ideally, it should begin right when you plan your venture.

What are your short-term and long-term goals? If your startup is to succeed, you should first define what success means to you. You should determine key performance indicators (KPIs), but make sure they're realistic. However, you shouldn't get hung up over KPIs. Dwell on a challenge instead.

Just like Sakichi Toyoda, state a challenge that you wish your startup will accomplish. Make sure the dare is bound to benefit a lot of people without directly causing damages and injuries.

Accomplish the challenge using courage and creativity. Don't be afraid of mistakes. They're going to happen no matter how careful you are. Even if you're using equipment, there can still be errors.

What if you don't have the equipment needed to meet the challenge? Let creativity take over. Make the most out of your workforce, but be sure to keep them well-compensated. Take advantage of free resources. Learn from your competitors' mistakes.

Lenders and angel investors are also there to provide financial backing to your startup. Have the guts to apply for loan or ask for funding from someone you know.

It may take years before you can accomplish the challenge. This means some of your attempts will end up in failures. However, those failures aren't fruitless at all. They can serve as training for both you and your team. They can also teach about what processes and changes don't bring out good results.

Once you succeed, create another challenge. You might not realize it but you're already applying kaizen at that point.

Notes:

- Focus on innovation, not on competition.

- Resistance, misconceptions and failure to determine important processes are obstruction against kaizen implementation.

- The three principles behind effective kaizen are processes and results, systemic thinking, and non-blaming.

- To start continuous improvement, determine and meet challenges.

- Courage and creativity help you meet challenges.

-

Resources:

Assembly. (2011, December 28). The Creators of Toyota's DNA. Retrieved November 3, 2019, from https://www.assemblymag.com/articles/8459 6-the-creators-of-toyota-s-dna

Boitnott, J. (2014, October 22). 6 Startups with the Most Humble Beginnings and the Greatest Successes. Retrieved November 3, 2019, from https://www.inc.com/john-boitnott/6-startups-with-the-most-humble-beginnings-and-the-greatest-successes.html

Bunkley, N. (2008, April 24). G.M. Says Toyota Has Lead in Global Sales Race. *The New York Times*. Retrieved from https://www.nytimes.com/2008/04/24/busine ss/worldbusiness/24auto.html?_r=3&ref=busi ness&oref=slogin&oref=slogin&oref=slogin

Donilon, T. (2019, August 14). Advantage, America. Retrieved November 3, 2019, from

https://www.foreignaffairs.com/articles/unite
d-states/2016-06-28/advantage-america

Hasegawa, Y., & Kimm, T. (2008). *Clean Car Wars: How Honda and Toyota are Winning the Battle of the Eco-Friendly Autos*. Chichester, United Kingdom: Wiley.

K. Liker, J. K., Hoseus, M., & Center for Quality People and Organizations. (2008). Toyota Culture: The Heart and Soul of the Toyota Way (Rev. ed.). United States of America: McGraw-Hill Education.

Magee, D. (2008). *How Toyota Became #1: Leadership Lessons from the World's Greatest Car Company* (Rev. ed.). New York, United States of America: Portfolio.

Organisation Internationale des Constructeurs d'Automobiles. (2017). *WORLD MOTOR VEHICLE PRODUCTION: OICA correspondents survey*. Retrieved from http://www.oica.net/wp-content/uploads/World-Ranking-of-Manufacturers-1.pdf

Rodrigues, E. (2018, November 7). How to overcome the Biggest Obstacles to Kaizen Implementation [Blog post]. Retrieved November 3, 2019, from https://prodsmart.com/blog/2018/11/07/how-to-overcome-the-biggest-obstacles-to-kaizen-implementation/

Rosenthal, M. (2011). The Essence of Jidoka. Retrieved November 3, 2019, from https://web.archive.org/web/20110714222919/http://www.sme.org/cgi-bin/get-newsletter.pl?LEAN&20021209&1&

Vlasic, B. (2011). *Once Upon a Car: The Fall and Resurrection of America's Big Three Automakers--GM, Ford, and Chrysler*. United States of America: HarperCollins.

Chapter 2: Relating Kaizen to Managing a Startup

"Great discoveries and improvements invariably involve the cooperation of many minds." (Alexander Graham Bell)

Kaizen is applicable to many aspects of business. After all, each aspect of business management requires continuous improvement.

Key Phrase: Important Business Process

So, your office's bathroom sink drains slowly every time someone uses it. Imagine the time and effort that some users devote in attempting to resolve the problem. Then, your employees spend more time complaining and suggesting instant remedies. When things get worse or when you see the problem yourself, perhaps you'll give it attention and hire a plumber yourself. How do you stop the problem from recurring? Are you also going to apply kaizen on it?

Obviously, you don't have to obsess over continuous improvement on your bathroom's functionality. There's no need as long as the bathroom is safe and sanitary, the fixtures are in good condition, and there are enough stalls and features for your employees.

Focus kaizen on important business processes. These processes differ from one industry to another. For manufacturers, the manufacturing procedure is clearly the most important one. If you're into retailing, providing choices, allowing customers to select, and processing orders forms part of the significant business process. Offering topnotch customer experience sum up the important process in the service industry.

A business process is basically the structured set of activities involved in delivering the product or service to customers. It involves creation, selection, payment and delivery. Under creation, you'll have to deal with supply management and quality control. Marketing forms part of providing choices for your customers. Payment involves accounting while delivery covers customer service.

By understanding your key business process, you can allocate your resources more effectively. You can also choose which business functions you should continuously improve. These are more manageable when you're operating a startup as the process tends to be simpler.

As your business grows, the business gets complicated. Aside from your main business process, there'll be management and supporting processes (Scheer, von Rosing & von Scheel, 2014).

Familiarizing yourself with your important business is pretty simple yet beneficial. Unfortunately, not a lot of aspiring and struggling entrepreneurs know this. Some of them add steps like gathering feedback and informing their customers about other products and services. If customers are rushing, the last thing they'll need is listening to an agent's marketing spiel.

Three Steps to Remember in Developing Kaizen Culture in the Workplace

Upon determining your key business process, you can initiate continuous improvement by performing three steps (Magee, 2007). The steps are as follows:

1. Identify problem.

2. Find out the root cause.

3. Formulate a solution.

The aforementioned steps don't look groundbreaking at all, do they? There are similarities with how doctors diagnose conditions and how students solve Math problems.

The difference of kaizen, however, is how it underscores the second step. This isn't to say that doctors don't exert effort in pinpointing the root cause of their patients' conditions. For kaizen's root cause analysis, you have to remember two concepts: the five whys and genchi genbutsu.

The Five Whys

The concept of five whys is basically about asking why for five times in order to reach the root cause of a problem (Ohno, 2006). This practice is applicable on business operations and even on your personal life.

Here's an example on applying five whys in your personal life:

1. Why did you oversleep? Because I was tired.

2. Why were you tired? Because I had to walk home.

3. Why did you have to walk home? Because I couldn't book a ride.

4. Why couldn't you book a ride? Because my phone broke.

5. Why did your phone break? Because the phone slipped and got dropped from my pocket.

Based on the above scenario, the root cause of oversleeping was dropping the phone. That appears illogical. But when you think about the root cause, you can assume that it has a lot to do with clumsiness and dependence on one's phone. Then, you develop a solution. It could be fixing the broken phone, buying a new one, or bringing a power bank.

Below is an example of applying the five whys in your business operations:

1. Why did customers refuse buying your products? Because your products weren't sealed.

2. Why were your products not sealed? Because the machine for sealing broke.

3. Why did the machine for sealing break? Because the seal got stuck in between the gears.

4. Why did seal get stuck in between the gears? Because the seal was too thick.

5. Why was the seal too thick? Because the wrong seal was used.

In the said scenario, the solution should cover removing the obstruction and replacing the wrong seal with the correct one. Once tested and fixed, make sure your products are sealed accordingly.

Don't try to dig deeper than the five whys. In the above scenario, asking another why is likely to give human error as the root cause. (This doesn't have to apply when you're trying out the five whys on a personal issue.) The analysis should never end up with such kind of root cause because you or your employees will blame one person.

Be mindful of your reasonings as well. Never jump into conclusions when asking each of the five whys. The answer to one of them should be a direct cause. For example, if you wonder why the machine broke, you shouldn't say it was because it's old. Wear and tear increase the risk of machine breakdowns. However, it's the damage they bring that could serve as direct cause to malfunctions.

The root cause shouldn't be another symptom of the problem as well. Going back to the aforementioned scenario about the machine, when you're answering why the seal got stuck, don't say it's because the machine also stopped the day before.

As much as possible, use a pen and paper (or marker and whiteboard) when asking and answering the five whys. Don't do it on your computer or phone. Otherwise, the autocorrect and autofill functions of your devices may end up doing the analysis for you. Writing, in contrast, gives you a bit more time dwelling on the possible causes. You can also do mind maps better when you do it on paper or whiteboard.

To realize if your root cause analysis is logical, one trick is to recite the answers minus the word because. Start from the answer for the fifth why. Afterwards, say "therefore" followed by the fourth answer. Repeat that until you reach the first answer. For the above scenario, your answers should be like the following: The wrong seal was used. Therefore, it was too thick for the machine's gears. Therefore, it got stuck in between the gears. Therefore, the machine for sealing broke. Therefore, the products weren't sealed.

Below are additional examples of applying root cause analysis specifically for managing a startup:

Scenario 1: Your ecommerce site has high traffic. However, your website's lead conversion rates are low.

1. Why were your lead conversion rates low? Because the majority of your leads didn't click the Buy button.

2. Why didn't the majority of your buyers click the Buy button? Because they didn't see it right away.

3. Why didn't they see it right away? Because the button didn't stand out.

4. Why didn't the button stand out? Because it was located far below the page.

5. Why was it located far below the page? Because it was placed below the lengthy product details and description.

Scenario 2: You're handing out flyers for your upcoming launch. However, you notice that the receivers throw them away in the nearest trash bin.

1. Why did the receivers throw away your flyers? Because you only forced them to receive flyers.

2. Why did you force them to receive the flyers? Because you didn't have enough time to distribute properly.

3. Why didn't you have enough time to distribute properly? Because you were rushing to distribute a box of flyers.

4. Why were you rushing to distribute a box of flyers? Because you printed a lot.

5. Why did you print a lot? Because you had plenty of unused paper and ink.

Scenario 3: You have a coffee shop in a busy street. You provide a selection of flavorful and affordable drinks, along with special and expensive ones. Queues are starting to become a normal sight in your establishment. While this looks like a sign of popularity, it can also be viewed as a problem that warrants a root cause analysis.

1. Why were there queues in your coffee shop? Because customers in front spent a lot of time ordering.

2. Why did the customers in front spend a lot of time ordering? Because they had to ask the available flavors, quantities and prices.

3. Why did they have to ask the available flavors, quantities and prices? Because they couldn't read your menu overhead.

4. Why couldn't they read your menu overhead? Because it was poorly lit.

5. Why was it poorly lit? Because there were too few light bulbs.

Scenario 4: You develop a food delivery app. After an upgrade, the number of users suddenly drop.

1. Why did the number of users suddenly drop after the upgrade? Because many of them chose other food delivery apps.

2. Why did many of them choose other food delivery apps? Because your app became confusing to use.

3. Why did your app become confusing to use? Because you changed the layout of your app's interface.

4. Why did you change the layout of your app's interface? Because you found it too plain.

5. Why did you find it too plain? Because it had no other functionalities aside from processing order and accepting payment.

Scenario 5: You already sent a customer's order. Afterwards, the customer complains about receiving the wrong product. You check your record and discovered the ordered and delivered products are the same. Instead of asking assurances from your customer that he didn't commit the mistake, consider doing the root cause analysis first.

1. Why did the wrong product get sent? Because the customer placed the wrong order.

2. Why did the customer place the wrong order? Because the packaging of the products looked the same.

3. Why did the packaging of the products look the same? Because you lacked designs.

4. Why did you lack designs? Because you didn't have much time designing packaging for other products.

5. Why didn't you have much time designing packaging for other products? Because their development and production were only given a month.

Genchi Genbutsu

Literally meaning "real location, real thing", genchi genbutsu serves as another guiding principle on how Toyota handles problem. The concept is fittingly known as go and see. After all, it encourages you to go to the problem's source and see it for yourself (Magee, 2007).

This is something that many startup owners should perform. Unlike big companies, you don't have many executives, supervisors and managers who have both the power and function to resolve issues in their respective areas. As a startup owner, you won't have many eyes and hands helping you spot problems.

Here's a simple example of applying genchi genbutsu: You notice a commotion in the restaurant you own and manage. It involves an angry customer talking down on a server. Instead of allowing the poor employee handle the brunt of the customer's emotion, step in and find out what it's all about. Make sure you ask both sides.

That sounds like a normal reaction for restaurant managers. However, there are managers who don't feel the need to do such an obvious task. Some even blame and shame their servers publicly.

If you're an app developer, you can apply genchi genbutsu when your users report bugs. You should download, install and use your app yourself. Do what the users did before they encountered the bugs. Experience how the bugs affect user experience. From there, you can ask the five whys and develop a solution afterwards.

Applying genchi genbutsu gets a little complex as your business expands. As you provide managerial powers to one or two employees, should you still go and see the problem yourself?

The answer is yes, especially if your employees are new to having managerial power. When you see the problem yourself, however, you shouldn't just observe and formulate your solutions right after.

Genchi genbutsu requires you to ask the employees who are working in the area where the problem originated. You can inquire about what happened right before the problem or the symptoms showed up. It's an integral step in collecting data at the actual site of the problem.

When everything in your business goes smoothly, you shouldn't settle down. Find a problem and treat it as a challenge. Moreover, think of it as a chance to improve. In the next chapter, you'll get a better understanding of the benefits of continuous improvement.

Notes:

- Before you aim for continuous improvement, determine your business's important process.

- The three steps in developing kaizen culture in the workplace are: identifying problem, finding out the root cause, and formulating a solution.

- To find out the root cause, ask five whys and apply genchi genbutsu.

- When asking five whys, make sure you're stating the direct cause for each why.

- Genchi genbutsu means go to the problem's source and see for yourself.

- Treat problem as a challenge and a chance for improvement.

Resources:

Magee, D. (2008). *How Toyota Became #1: Leadership Lessons from the World's Greatest Car Company* (Rev. ed.). New York, United States of America: Portfolio.

Ohno, T. (2006, March). "Ask 'why' five times about every matter." Retrieved November 3, 2019, from https://www.toyota-myanmar.com/about-toyota/toyota-traditions/quality/ask-why-five-times-about-every-matter

Von Rosing, M., Von Scheel, H., & Scheer, A. W. (2014). *The Complete Business Process Handbook: Body of Knowledge from Process Modeling to BPM*. United States of America: Elsevier Science.

Chapter 3: Highlighting the Benefits of Kaizen

"Isn't it funny how day by day nothing changes but when you look back, everything is different?" (C. S. Lewis)

Kaizen is instrumental in shaping Toyota's legacy. The same could happen to your startup if you and your employees fully embrace the concept. But before you start thinking of becoming the frontrunner in your industry, below are the benefits you should expect from doing continuous improvement.

Effective Management-Employee Communication

This is both a requirement and a benefit of applying kaizen. You need effective communication to instill your goals and strategies to your employees. You also need that in collecting information about problems and in getting feedback for the changes you introduce.

Teaching your goals and strategies right from the start helps ensure that you and your employees stay on the same page as you expand your business. This also gives your employees insights on the possible career growth they can have with your startup. Having such insights let them consider if they're going to stay with you for a long time.

Eliminating the blame game and encouraging them to inform you about problems speed up crisis management. These actions, along with allowing them to give feedback, boost their confidence and make them feel less stressed at work.

According to the Canadian Centre for Occupational Health and Safety, work-related stress causes short-term effects like headaches, chest pains and muscle tensions. It can badly affect sleep as well. This further causes employees to make poor judgment and neglect their duties at work. Such effects mean losses on your part. Imagine paying for their time, but not getting the work you required them to do.

In contrast, having a great workplace environment makes employees want to work better and stay longer. This can also be beneficial in your branding efforts later on.

Furthermore, effective communication is needed in reviewing your kaizen efforts. This turns into advantage as you or your employees can alert about the possibility of getting sidetracked. The sooner you realize it, the sooner you can work your way back to accomplishing your goals.

Elimination of the Seven Types of Waste

A complex manufacturing procedure and product surplus make it look like your business is doing well. Does your revenue increase though? Are you able to achieve your long-term goals as well?

What seem like signs of business doing well are actually forms of waste. As they're kinds of waste, it's only right to eliminate them. To eliminate them, you should be able to identify them first. According to Ohno (1988), there are seven types of waste in the business process. You can remember them as TIM WOOD.

1. Transport

From the delivery of raw materials to the shipment of finished products, several movements are involved. In the case of manufacturing food products, the steps include cleaning produce, processing, packing, labeling and warehousing. The plant should be organized with the first station being the cleaning area. Next to it should be the processing area, followed by the packing and labeling stations. The next should be near the entrance to the warehouse.

Organizing that way is a no-brainer. However, one of the common mistakes of inexperienced manufacturers is that they organize with maximizing space in mind. They try to fill as much space as possible. Others focus on keeping manual labor in one part, while the steps involving machines are on another area.

A problematic workplace setup creates the transport waste. This type of waste refers to the unnecessary movement of products. Aside from wasting time, the unnecessary movement puts your products at risk of mishandling. They may get misplaced as well. The complex setup may also cause collisions between workers.

2. Inventory

Raw materials, work in progress and finished products signify costs until they're delivered to the consumers. After all, you're paying for the supply of raw materials, the electricity for powering up machines, the delivery of your products to consumers and the labor needed to carry out the steps in your business process.

If you store excessive raw materials, unfinished products, and finished ones, you're bound to deal with the second type of waste: inventory. The surplus is deemed as a waste because warehousing alone costs money but doesn't give you anything in return. Perhaps, you can say it gives you assurance that you can use the extras in case there's a disruption in your production. But there's also the possibility that, when a finished product is discovered to be defective, that means you're less likely to sell your surplus unless you lower the costs.

Moreover, if there are no disruptions in your production processes and the demand for your products remains the same, the surplus will stay in your warehouse for a long time. Some manufacturers end up offering the extras as bundles just to clear their warehouses. The "buy 1, take 1" marketing strategy seems like a good one until you realize how you have to reduce the price to get rid of surplus.

3. Motion

The third type of waste happens when the equipment and workers are inefficient in what they're supposed to do. It's somewhat related to the transport waste. Their main difference though is that transport waste is about damages from moving products, while motion waste is about the damages from the workers and equipment that directly make the products.

Wear-and-tear damage in equipment is a classic example of motion waste. Equipment breakdowns are another example. You can also consider overworked and injured workers.

4. Waiting

Also known as delays and idle time, the fourth type is all about wasted time in the production process. Waiting can happen when you're understaffed or when work is poorly distributed.

Excessive delays in the production are bound to adversely affect your delivery of goods. Consequently, they can result to complaints and cancellation of orders.

5. Overproduction

Dubbed as the worst type of waste (Perrin, 2015), overproduction can trigger and worsen the other six. As its name suggests, this refers to the excessive production of goods when there is low or even no demand at all.

Overproduction is the number one cause of inventory problem. If you don't address the overproduction problem, you're going to worsen your inventory waste. Disposing the surplus means additional work later on.

Instead of delivering newly finished products to retailers or to the consumers, you may also end up storing them for the meantime and shipping the surplus from the previous production. This becomes a form of transport waste.

As a remedy to the surplus, you may lower production in the next few days or weeks. This means some of your employees will free up some of the work time you're paying them for.

Overproduction can trigger quality control problems as well. This is especially true if you're in the food manufacturing industry. When you're storing the excess, you need to be more mindful of expiry dates. Otherwise, they may end up rotting in your warehouse.

6. Over Processing

Front and back cameras are one of the advantageous features of smartphones. One in front and another one at the back are enough. Why add more? Shouldn't phone manufacturers just improve the quality and features of dual cams instead?

Such is just an example of over processing. Adding the extra camera means costs and another step in the production process. Perhaps, the only advantage of having such is that when one camera breaks, you can still have a couple left. You won't feel the need to fix the broken cam. But, as it is a feature you paid for, will you just leave it like that?

Over processing refers to the addition of unnecessary steps in your production. This waste also covers the use of raw materials that are more expensive and of higher quality than what you required for your production. If you're ordering the materials from overseas despite having local suppliers, you'll also deal with over processing, transport, and waiting waste.

7. Defect

Out of all the types of waste, defects are the easiest to understand. Defective products mean you can't recoup your expenses for their production. You wasted time, raw materials, electricity, and your workers' efforts. Depending on the severity of the defects, the goods could be considered literal waste as well.

It's only right to issue recall for defective goods. If you refuse to do so, you risk good reputation. Moreover, you lose loyal customers in the process. But just like Toyota's journey, it's still possible to bounce back and become better than before.

Getting rid of the seven types of waste helps you maximize your resources. Consider the reduced operational costs. You can use the capital you saved for paying loans or for investing on necessary equipment. When it comes to labor, you can use the waiting time for training in a more advanced work.

Eliminating waste is one of the objectives of lean manufacturing. Lean is basically a methodology. It involves streamlining your processes.

By knowing the seven types of waste, identifying areas you need to improve on becomes more manageable. The term lean kaizen denotes an approach of ensuring continuous improvement and eliminating waste.

The production is the most crucial step in a business process. In the case of providing software, the development phase is the most important part. If you're offering services, training and customer service are the most essential. In these steps, you can actually find the abovementioned types of waste. For service providers though, the defect refers to unsatisfactory work while overproduction may be equated to extensive service hours without extra charge.

Some types of waste can also be found in other business functions. You can relate them even in the administrative work that doesn't have direct involvement with products and customers. Delays and inefficient employees (motion waste) are the two common types of waste in non-production steps in your business process. Below are some examples:

- Keeping several boxes of printing paper for administrative work is an example of inventory waste.

- Erroneous data in reports is a form of defect.

- Buying, using and maintaining the most expensive computers when there are affordable and equally efficient options form part of over processing waste.

- Printing more flyers than necessary is an example of overproduction.

Safer Work Environment

With effective communication, your employees can inform you about health risks in the workplace. You can address them right away to avoid accidents. While it's true that your insurance may cover hospitalization costs of an injured employee, nothing can protect your startup from the backlash from the other employees. If news of the accident becomes public, you'll earn bad reputation as well. The results are worse when there's death involved.

Instead of the repercussions of workplace accidents though, you should ensure safer workplace because it's only ethical. Your workforce is a valuable resource. As a resource, you should give them an environment that helps them maximize their performance, and protects them. Value them and make them feel valued.

Better Customer Experience

As an entrepreneur, you shouldn't think you're only offering products or services. You should keep in mind that you're providing customer experience.

Many products these days are more of luxuries, not necessities. Smart TV is one of the notable examples. It's mainly for entertainment. You can use it for video conferences, too. However, a smartphone or high-tech laptop can be enough for such task.

Yet, people still buy smart TVs because it allows them to watch live broadcasts of games. The bigger screen and better video quality make them feel like they're part of the audience.

Some smart TV ads show a family watching together or one adult relaxing on the couch. They're basically selling the experience you can have when you use the product.

Luxury bags are worth noting as well. Some ladies just want them because the brands make them feel like they're members of the elite. The bags can also give them the notion of elegance.

How about your offer? What kind of experience do you wish your customer will have when using your product or getting your service?

Lean kaizen helps you improve the customer experience you can provide. The continuously improving product is the biggest reason. Having confident and efficient employees, especially those who directly deal with customers, is another factor.

Notes:

- Kaizen needs and enhances effective communication between management and employees.

- Kaizen helps eliminate the seven types of waste in the business process. These types of waste are transport, inventory, motion, waiting, overproduction, over processing, and defect.

- Kaizen can help ensure a safe and efficient work environment.

- Thanks to continuously improving product and service, you can give better customer experience.

Resources:

Canadian Centre for Occupational Health and Safety. (n.d.). Workplace Stress - General. Retrieved November 3, 2019, from https://www.ccohs.ca/oshanswers/psychosocial/stress.html

Ohno, T. (1988). *Toyota Production System: Beyond Large-Scale Production* (Rev. ed.). United States of America: Taylor & Francis.

Perrin, X. (2015, January 4). Why is Overproduction the Worst Muda? Retrieved November 3, 2019, from http://www.consulting-xp.com/blog/?p=546

Chapter 4: Applying Kaizen in Managing a Startup

"The man who moves a mountain begins by carrying away small stones." (Confucius)

Fostering kaizen culture in your workplace won't happen just because you want to. It requires effort, consistency, patience and cooperation. To overcome resistance, you also have to start small. People are more receptive to minor changes after all.

You also have to follow the 5S program to make your workplace environment conducive to kaizen and to help ensure that the changes last for a long time. While this was developed for Toyota's manufacturing procedure, this has been adapted for other steps in the business process. The 5S were originally Japanese words but they had English counterparts as they became one of the bases of lean manufacturing.

The 5S to Remember

1. Sort (Seiri)

This step is about differentiating what's valuable and what's not. To carry this out, you have to go to the location and find out what doesn't belong.

Under the first S, you have to identify obstructions. You need to ensure safety and maximize resources, particularly time, space and manpower.

You can accomplish the said goals by removing obstructions unless these have a lot do with the structure of your workplace. You can ask an interior designer to help you redo your workplace's floor plan in such a way that doesn't involve demolitions. But if the obstructions are furniture or equipment, you can rearrange them.

Collect items that don't belong in certain areas, too. Compile them in all on a table or in a corner. Put them in their respective areas later on.

Try to put yourself in the shoes of your employees as well. They should be able to move comfortably in the workplace. They shouldn't have to squeeze their way through. Maximizing space doesn't have to mean filling every square inch. The freed space can serve as wider walkway. A more spacious walkway helps prevent collisions and speed up transfer of goods.

2. Set in order/Straighten (Seiton)

This refers to putting things in their respective places. If the first S focuses on what to be eliminated, the second one underscores keeping the needed equipment and employees where they're supposed to be. Its goal is to make sure the workflow goes as smoothly as possible.

To implement this, make sure you have the needed work stations to perform key steps in your business process. They should be positioned in such a way that limits delays and transport waste. Next, fill the work stations with the right equipment and people. Even the storage for the equipment and supplies should be within those work stations.

3. Shine (Seiso)

Basically, this concept is about maintaining cleanliness and ensuring that your equipment is in optimal condition. Maintenance is needed because it also helps ensure the safety of your employees.

Inspection of equipment and procedure is an integral step in the third S. Random visits in your employees' respective work stations are also recommended.

4. Standardize (Seiketsu)

This step is all about creating rules and summing up your procedures. Defining such makes your employees understand what they need to do. This also involves modifying steps.

5. Sustain (Shitsuke)

It's pointless to improve a step then revert back to your old ways. The final step aims to prevent that from happening. Sustaining is about maintaining and aiming for improvement over and over.

Application of 5S in Production

What do your customers say about your product? As a startup, you can give your initial set of products to a control group. Take note of the negative feedback. Compile them and identify the most complained about issue. Ask the five whys and go to the area in the production where the problem first occurred.

From there, sort out the things that aren't meant in the area and bring the tools you needed for the job. Repair whatever needs to be repaired. Modify the wrongful step that trigger the flaw in your product's design or functionality. Maintain the new procedure. If that doesn't fix the problem with your product, go back to the modifications you introduced.

Going back to the sample problem of unsealed products, the first thing you should do is remove the box of wrong seal. Next, bring the box of correct seal in the packing area. The third step is to inspect and repair the machine. The employee concerned should be alerted about the problem as well. To avoid repeating the mistake, the employees in-charge of supplies should double-check if they're of the correct size. Sustain it by adding the said task for every transaction.

Introducing Kaizen Board

Search for productivity tips in Pinterest and Google Images. There's a great chance that you'll see boards with three columns known as To-Do, Doing and Done (Kniberg & Skarin, 2010). Over the years, people put their own spin on the said productivity tool. There are even apps based on it. Such tool is actually called the kanban board.

Ohno (1988) also developed the scheduling system known as kanban. The main difference between kanban and kaizen is that the former focuses more on logistics while kaizen puts a lot of emphasis on people and improvements. Yet, both can be used together. The kaizen board is a fusion of the two.

The Rationale Behind a Kaizen Board

You and your employees shouldn't wait for problems and their symptoms to occur before you carry out root cause analysis and solutions. However, encouraging your employees to find trouble isn't as easy as it seems.

Sometimes, you have to set up a reminder for you and for them to spot possible problems. That's what a kaizen board does. Aside from identifying progress, this tool lets you see the progress for the changes you introduce.

Tips on Designing and Using a Kaizen Board

The basic kaizen board has four columns. The first one is entitled the Idea column. It's followed by To-Do, Doing and Done.

Your kaizen board doesn't have to be fancy. You can use a pinboard or a whiteboard. To put entries under each column, you can use sticky notes, memo pads, or simply pens.

Make sure employees (even the lowest in the ranks and temporary ones) have a say on what you need to improve on in your startup, main offer, and management style. To make this possible, the kaizen board should be visible in the workplace.

The board should be at least 2 square feet. The ideal place is also near the entryway or the lounge.

Keep the pens, sticky notes, memo pads and pins right beside or under the board. Add a note encouraging your employees to use the said materials to enter their suggestions in the Ideas column.

Afterwards, organize a weekly meeting to process the Ideas. It can be as short as 30 minutes, but make sure it's part of the work period, not on breaks. If you do it on breaks, your employees may not treat your kaizen board seriously.

During those meetings, you can also update the kaizen board. Those in-charge of planning and working on certain ideas should provide entries in the To-Do and Doing sections respectively. If the work is finished, there should be updates on the Done column. The entries in the Done column should be kept for at least a week.

If you have more than 20 employees, you should provide a separate kaizen board for each team. Consider the number of members for each team when deciding the size of the kaizen board. You can collectively discuss the ideas from the different kaizen boards. But if your business starts to branch out and have more teams, separate discussions are better.

If your business is into software development, you can further modify the kaizen board by adding Testing column in between the To-Do and Doing columns. The Testing column is beneficial when you have two or more ways of accomplishing the To-Do entries.

Notes:

- Remember the 5S: sort, set in order, shine, standardize and sustain.

- Make a kaizen board to generate ideas.

Resources:

Kniberg, H., & Skarin, M. (2010). *Kanban and Scrum: Making the Most of Both*. United States of America: C4Media Inc.

Ohno, T. (1988). *Toyota Production System: Beyond Large-Scale Production* (Rev. ed.). United States of America: Taylor & Francis.

Conclusion

I'd like to thank you and congratulate you for transiting my lines from start to finish.

I hope this book was able to help you in carrying out kaizen in your startup business. The management approach is based on both scientific evidences and common sense. It's not that surprising that you can apply it regardless of the industry you're in, the location of your business and the nationality of your employees.

Additionally, kaizen is applicable no matter how small your business is. It's even more ideal for startups than large corporations. The former has limited capital for funding operations, after all. Streamlining the business process helps a startup save and utilize the savings for further improvements.

Hopefully, this was able to help you appreciate the importance of teamwork as well. It's been reiterated many times how valuable that factor is. However, some people who attain success tend to think they're able to do so without anyone's help. As a result, the people who helped turned their backs against them.

Part of being a good entrepreneur is managing human resource well. Give them the support they need. You can start with moral support. Encourage and reassure them as a group. Ensure them a safe environment. Afterwards, train them in handling new tasks and taking leadership roles.

Don't forget to pay them well. This may mean increasing your operation costs and reducing your profit. However, the long-term benefits may include employee satisfaction and loyalty. Satisfied employees can promote your brand without asking for additional payment from you. Your customers will consider them more reliable as they've been with you for quite long.

Moreover, you can further attract skilled people if you know how to recognize hard work. However, you shouldn't distinguish individual efforts.

By introducing you to kaizen, I hope you're also able to identify your key business process. Remove the steps that don't add value to the way you serve your customers. Refining your business process is bound to improve your customers' experience with your brand. To help you decide whether a change or an existing step forms part of your key business process, ask yourself, "How does it benefit my customer?"

Continuous improvement doesn't have a definite ending, which is a good thing because you'll keep on striving for it. While it doesn't have an ending, it always begins with a challenge.

Long-term goals can be broken down into manageable challenges. Aside from that, you can use a kaizen board to generate ideas for challenges and set reminders for changes.

You can also try to spot the seven types of waste in all aspects of your business operation. To get rid of the seven types of waste, you should perform the following:

- Get rid of unnecessary steps in your business process.

- Avoid buying and storing extra materials.

- Strive to simplify complex steps.

- Invest on equipment and talents.

- Don't make more than what your customers need.

- Don't do more than your customers want.

- Avoid mistakes in the production.

Market analysis is required to carry out some of the above steps. Get to know the potential demand and the features that your target customers are hoping for. You can conduct an online survey, A/B testing, and interviews. You can study the leading ventures in your industry. Assess what features their products or services that don't add value to customers, and make sure they won't form part of your own offers.

Feedback forms and customer review sections in your site are also gold mines for possible challenges. During your meetings, you can also collect information about potential issues from your employees.

Part of teaching your employees about kaizen is training them to consider challenge as an opportunity for improvement. After determining a challenge, ask the five whys. Go to the source of the problem and consult the employees concerned as well.

After determining the root cause, develop a solution and implement them using the 5S: Sort; Set in order; Shine; Standardize; and Sustain. Get rid of the waste in the area where the problem started. Keep the needed equipment and people in the said area. Inspect and do necessary repairs. Train the workers there as well. Afterwards, modify the procedures to prevent the possible recurrence of the problem. Finally, sustain the newly introduced changes.

To test the 5S, try organizing your computer's desktop. Remove files, folders and programs in your desktop that you don't use for work.

For the second S, put the folders and programs you use for work on the desktop or taskbar. Compile important files in properly labelled folders as well. Buy the necessary program licenses, too.

Next, scan your work folders and programs for possible malware. Delete useless files and folders as well.

Every time you use your computer, you may create and save new clutter in your desktop. Make sure you sort, set in order, and shine before you shut down your computer. This way, you're standardizing and sustaining the organized desktop.

From organizing your desktop, try out the 5S in decluttering your work desk. From there, apply them in your office or shop.

Just like Toyota, don't settle. Keep on improving your main offer, workforce, work environment, customer service and marketing strategies. Continue refining your processes. You may still incur losses along the way, but they won't last long if you aim for improvements.

It can take time. Your competitors may take the lead as you keep on improving. You may fall behind the trends. However, you should remember that leads and trends aren't permanent. If you aim for kaizen, you might become the next Toyota that introduced the hybrid age in your own industry. It's better to set the trends than follow, right?

The next step is to commit yourself on improving. Do it, not just for your venture, but also for your life. Encourage your employees to do the same.

Don't worry about failures. There are more things you can learn from failures than from successes. Make sure you keep records of what failed so you won't have to repeat them again.

I wish you the best of luck! Don't forget to celebrate your successes but don't let them get into your head.

Thank you

Before you go, I just wanted to say thank you for purchasing my book.

You could have picked from dozens of other books on the same topic but you took a chance and chose this one.

So, a HUGE thanks to you for getting this book and for reading all the way to the end.

Now I wanted to ask you for a small favor. *Could you please consider posting a review on the platform? Reviews are one of the easiest ways to support the work of independent authors.*

This feedback will help me continue to write the type of books that will help you get the results you want. So if you enjoyed it, please let me know!

Resources

Assembly. (2011, December 28). The Creators of
Toyota's DNA. Retrieved November 3, 2019,
from
https://www.assemblymag.com/articles/845
96-the-creators-of-toyota-s-dna

Boitnott, J. (2014, October 22). 6 Startups With the
Most Humble Beginnings and the Greatest
Successes. Retrieved November 3, 2019,
from https://www.inc.com/john-boitnott/6-
startups-with-the-most-humble-beginnings-
and-the-greatest-successes.html

Bunkley, N. (2008, April 24). G.M. Says Toyota Has
Lead in Global Sales Race. *The New York
Times*. Retrieved from
https://www.nytimes.com/2008/04/24/bus
iness/worldbusiness/24auto.html?_r=3&ref
=business&oref=slogin&oref=slogin&oref=sl
ogin

Canadian Centre for Occupational Health and
Safety. (n.d.). Workplace Stress - General.
Retrieved November 3, 2019, from
https://www.ccohs.ca/oshanswers/psychoso
cial/stress.html

Donilon, T. (2019, August 14). Advantage, America. Retrieved November 3, 2019, from https://www.foreignaffairs.com/articles/united-states/2016-06-28/advantage-america

Hasegawa, Y., & Kimm, T. (2008). *Clean Car Wars: How Honda and Toyota are Winning the Battle of the Eco-Friendly Autos*. Chichester, United Kingdom: Wiley.

K. Liker, J. K., Hoseus, M., & Center for Quality People and Organizations. (2008). *Toyota Culture: The Heart and Soul of the Toyota Way* (Rev. ed.). United States of America: McGraw-Hill Education.

Kniberg, H., & Skarin, M. (2010). *Kanban and Scrum: Making the Most of Both*. United States of America: C4Media Inc.

Magee, D. (2008). *How Toyota Became #1: Leadership Lessons from the World's Greatest Car Company* (Rev. ed.). New York, United States of America: Portfolio.

Ohno, T. (1988). *Toyota Production System: Beyond Large-Scale Production* (Rev. ed.). United States of America: Taylor & Francis.

Ohno, T. (2006, March). "Ask 'why' five times about every matter." Retrieved November 3, 2019, from https://www.toyota-myanmar.com/about-toyota/toyota-traditions/quality/ask-why-five-times-about-every-matter

Organisation Internationale des Constructeurs d'Automobiles. (2017). *WORLD MOTOR VEHICLE PRODUCTION: OICA correspondents survey*. Retrieved from http://www.oica.net/wp-content/uploads/World-Ranking-of-Manufacturers-1.pdf

Perrin, X. (2015, January 4). Why is Overproduction the Worst Muda? Retrieved November 3, 2019, from http://www.consulting-xp.com/blog/?p=546

Rodrigues, E. (2018, November 7). How to overcome the Biggest Obstacles to Kaizen Implementation [Blog post]. Retrieved November 3, 2019, from https://prodsmart.com/blog/2018/11/07/how-to-overcome-the-biggest-obstacles-to-kaizen-implementation/

Rosenthal, M. (2011). The Essence of Jidoka. Retrieved November 3, 2019, from https://web.archive.org/web/201107142229

19/http://www.sme.org/cgi-bin/get-newsletter.pl?LEAN&20021209&1&

Toyota. (n.d.). Toyota Way 2001. Retrieved November 3, 2019, from https://www.toyota-global.com/company/history_of_toyota/75years/data/conditions/philosophy/toyotaway2001.html

Vlasic, B. (2011). *Once Upon a Car: The Fall and Resurrection of America's Big Three Automakers--GM, Ford, and Chrysler.* United States of America: HarperCollins.

Von Rosing, M., Von Scheel, H., & Scheer, A. W. (2014). *The Complete Business Process Handbook: Body of Knowledge from Process Modeling to BPM.* United States of America: Elsevier Science.

www.ingramcontent.com/pod-product-compliance
Lightning Source LLC
Chambersburg PA
CBHW071441210326
41597CB00020B/3889